Danse Macabr
and Other Works for Solo Piano

Camille Saint-Saëns

Selected and with an Introduction by
Victor Rangel-Ribeiro

DOVER PUBLICATIONS, INC.
Mineola, New York

Bibliographical Note

This Dover edition, first published in 1999, is a new compilation of music originally published separately by Durand & Cie, Paris. Original publications were undated with the exception of the following titles: *Thême varié,* Op. 97, 1894; *Six études pour la main gauche seule,* Op. 135, 1912; and Liszt's transcription of *Danse macabre,* Op. 40, 1921.
The annotated contents list and main headings, with new English translations, are newly added. Victor Rangel-Ribeiro's introduction was prepared specially for this edition.

International Standard Book Number: 0-486-40409-9

Manufactured in the United States of America
Dover Publications, Inc., 31 East 2nd Street, Mineola, N.Y. 11501

INTRODUCTION

Who in their right mind would give a six-year-old boy the complete orchestral score of Mozart's *Don Giovanni* as a present, and expect the child to read through the two bound volumes right away? Camille Saint-Saëns, aged six, did receive just such a present from an admirer of his immense talent, and promptly read the opera through, cover to cover, not just once but several times, until he had the music memorized. Never was such an improbable present so much loved—and turn out to be so very appropriate!

If young Camille was neither as dazzling a child prodigy nor as exploited as his idol Mozart, his mother must take the blame for it, or the credit—for his father had died when the child was not quite two months old. He was such a sickly baby that on a doctor's advice he spent the first two years of his life away from his mother and great-aunt, being cared for by a nurse. Yet, consider the promise: shown a piano at age two, Camille at once took to it. He finished an entire course of study within a month, and soon began to improvise. By age four he had begun scribbling down notation. By age six he had already composed several pieces, and persuaded a woman singer to perform one of his songs—all twelve bars of it with a four-bar *ritornello*—while he himself solemnly accompanied her at the piano. The singer's father, impressed by what he heard, then came up with the gift of the Mozart score.

Saint-Saëns made his debut as piano soloist with orchestra at age ten, performing Beethoven's third piano concerto and a Mozart concerto in B-flat. In an essay entitled "Memories of My Childhood," he explains what followed: "After my first concert, which was a brilliant success, my teacher wanted me to give others, but my mother did not wish me to have a career as an infant prodigy. She had higher ambitions and was unwilling for me to continue in concert work for fear of injuring my health. The result was that a coolness sprang up between my teacher and me which ended our relations."

However, the youngster continued his studies at the pianoforte, reading everything he could lay his hands on. That included all of Beethoven's sonatas, which led a friend to protest to the mother, asking, "What music will he play when he is twenty?"

Prophetically, she answered: "He will play his own."

Saint-Saëns' early composition teacher was a man called Maleden, who taught a system where (according to Saint-Saëns) "the chords are not considered in and for themselves—as fifths, sixths, sevenths—but in relation to the pitch of the scale on which they appear. The chords acquire different characteristics according to the place they occupy, and, as a result, certain things are explained which are, otherwise, inexplicable."

Saint-Saëns by his own account was a rather intractable pupil, and this exposed him to Maleden's own unique method of arriving at a concensus. "Our lessons were often very stormy," the composer recalled later in life. "From time to time certain questions came up on which I could not agree with him. He would then take me quietly by the ear, bend my head and hold my ear to the table for a minute or two. Then, he would ask whether I had changed my mind. As I had not, he would think it over and very often he would confess that I was right."

Entering the conservatoire shortly after, at age twelve, Saint-Saëns soon established himself as an organist, carrying off first prize three years later. He then entered Jacques Halévy's composition class. But though Halévy himself had won the Prix de Rome, that prestigious prize eluded the young Camille no matter how hard he tried. Berlioz explained away the failure by quipping: "He had everything it takes, but lacked inexperience!"

Camille Saint-Saëns was born on October 9, 1835, far enough back in the nineteenth century to enjoy the patronage of Rossini, and lived to December 16, 1921—long enough to have had to endure and survive the abusive slings and arrows flung at him in his old age by a young and insolent Erik Satie. The old lion got his revenge, overshadowing his tormentor even in death. And his reputation endures. True, Saint-Saëns' music does not stir our emotions to the extent that Beethoven's does; he does not lead us to plumb the depths of despair, turning then to raise our spirits to the point of ecstasy. What he does, however, he does extremely well; his music, though light-hearted, cannot be taken lightly. It demands that the performer bring to it a verve, dexterity, and panache, and also a certain *joie de vivre;* it leaves us stimulated sometimes, and pleased and amused sometimes, and almost always it leaves us satisfied.

—Victor Rangel-Ribeiro

CONTENTS

Danse macabre, Op. 40 • *Dance of death* (1874) 1
Symphonic poem, transcribed for piano by Franz Liszt (1876)

Six études pour le piano, Op. 52 • *Six piano studies* (1877) 23
    1. Prélude   23
    2. Pour l'indépendance des doigts • *For finger independence*   28
    3. Prelude and Fugue in F minor   30
    4. Étude de rythme • *Rhythm study*   38
    5. Prelude and Fugue in A major   42
    6. En forme de valse • *In waltz form*   50

Allegro appassionato, Op. 70 (1884) 65

Album pour piano, Op. 72 • *Piano album* (1884) 78
    1. Prélude   78
    2. Carillon   83
    3. Toccata   87
    4. Valse • *Waltz*   93
    5. Chanson napolitaine • *Neapolitan song*   105
    6. Finale   111

Rhapsodie d'Auvergne, Op. 73 • *Auvergne rhapsody* (1884) 123

Wedding Cake, *Caprice-Valse*, Op. 76 (1885) 141
Originally for piano and orchestra / Transcribed for solo piano by A. Benfeld

Thème varié, Op. 97 • *Varied theme* (1894) 156

Three waltzes 168
    Valse mignonne, Op. 104 • *Dainty waltz* (1896)   168
    Valse langoureuse, Op. 120 • *Languid waltz* (1903)   174
    Valse gaie, Op. 139 • *Gay waltz* (1913)   182

***From* Six études pour le piano, Op. 111** • *Six piano studies* (1899) 194
    3. Prelude and Fugue in E-flat Minor   194
    4. "Les cloches de Las Palmas" • *"The bells of Las Palmas"*   200
    6. Toccata   206

Six études pour la main gauche seule, Op. 135
• *Six studies for left hand alone* (1912) 219
    1. Prélude   219
    2. Alla fuga • *In fugal style*   223
    3. Moto perpetuo • *Perpetual motion*   227
    4. Bourrée   232
    5. Élégie • *Elegy*   239
    6. Gigue   244

Danse macabre

Dance of death • Op. 40 (1874)

Symphonic poem, transcribed for piano by Franz Liszt (1876)

Un poco moderato

18   *Danse macabre*

SIX ÉTUDES POUR LE PIANO

Six piano studies • Op. 52 (1877)

To Monsieur Édouard Marlois

Prélude

Op. 52, No. 1

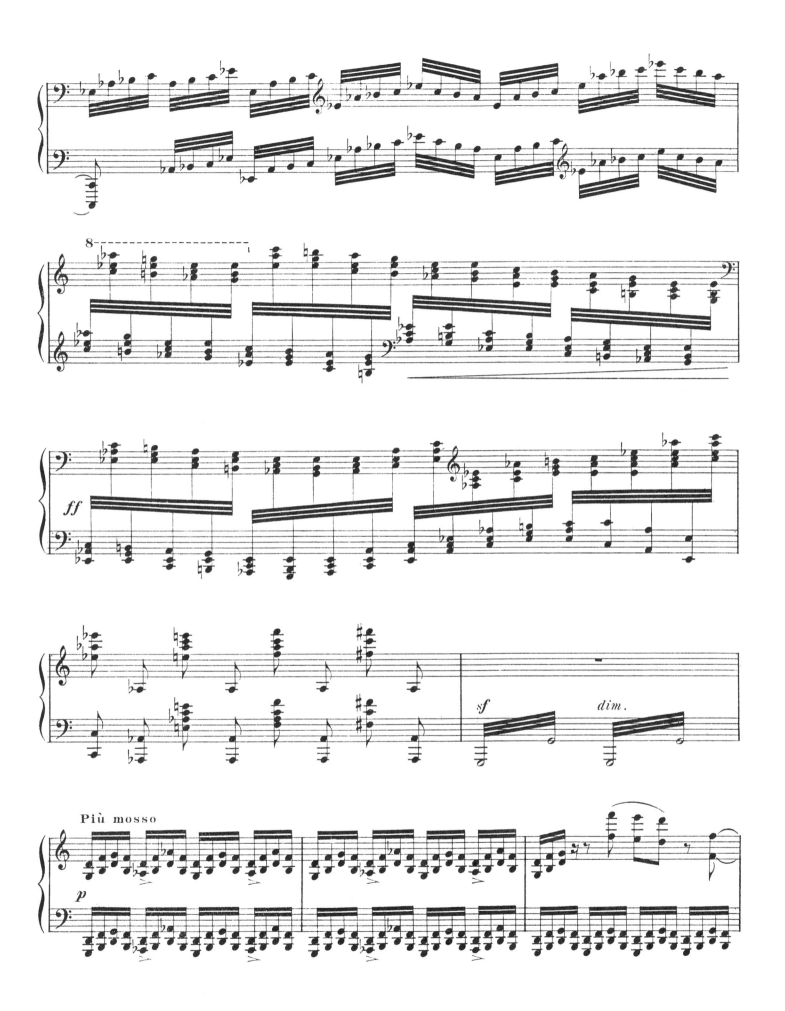

Pour l'indépendance des doigts

For finger independence • Op. 52, No. 2

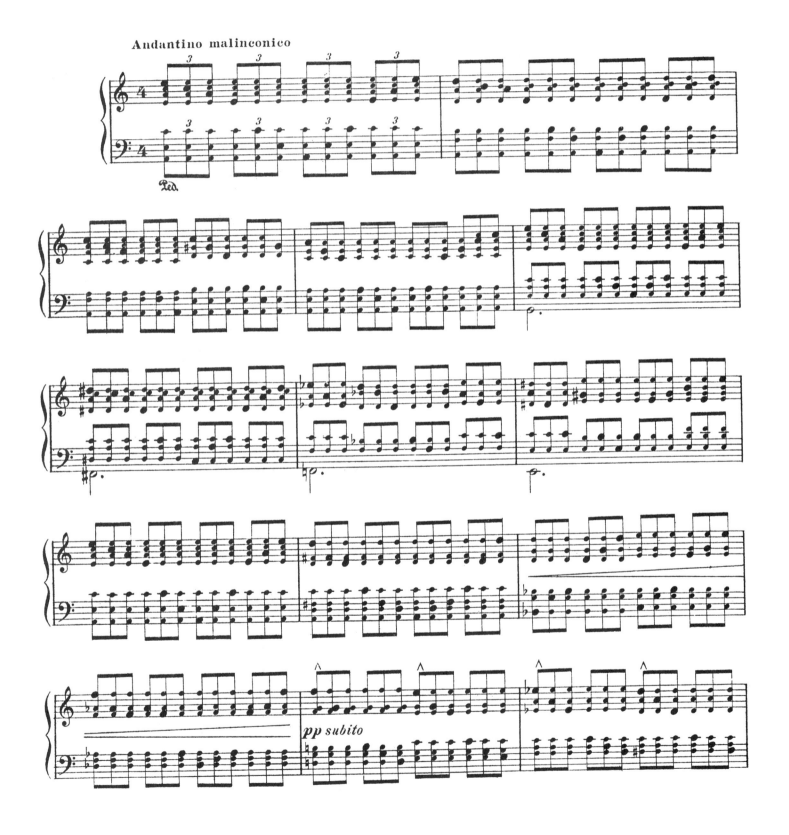

Prelude and Fugue in F minor

Op. 52, No. 3

PRÉLUDE

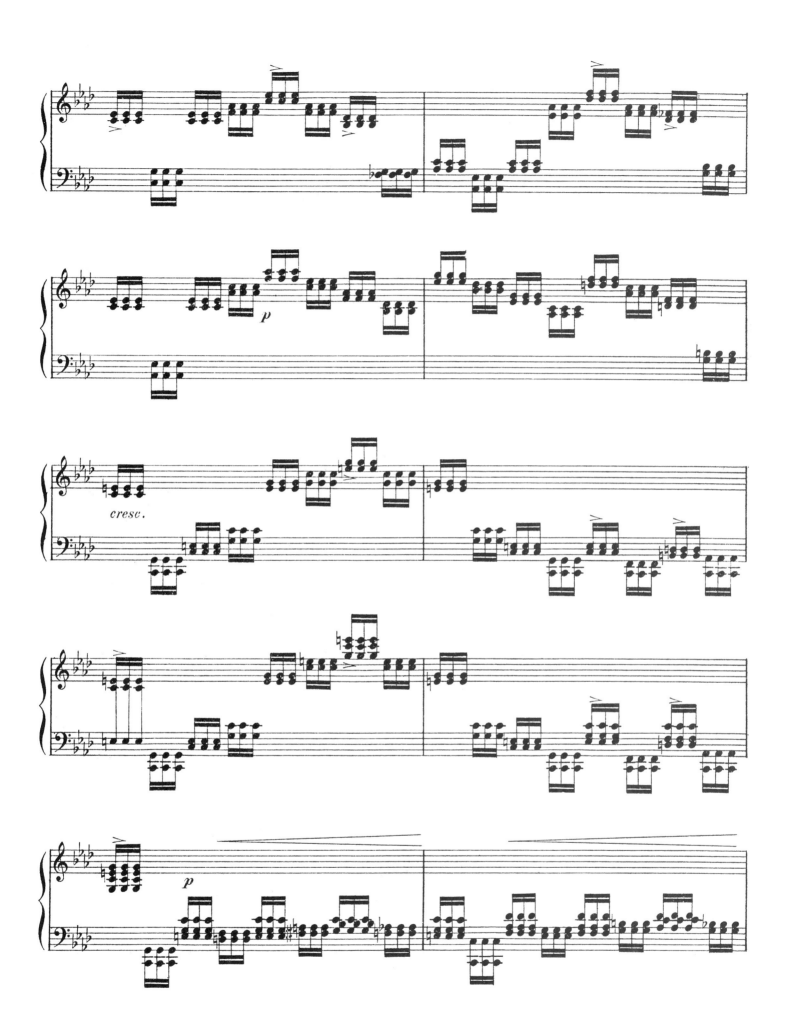

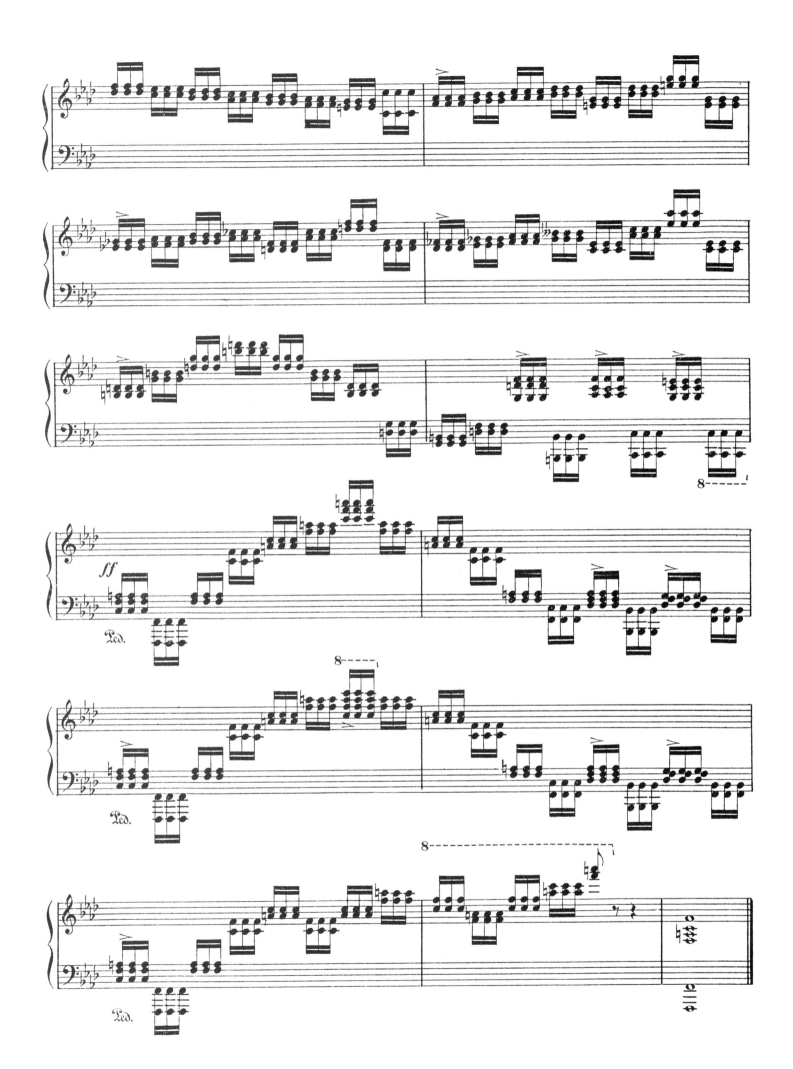

FUGUE

Étude de rythme

Rhythm study • Op. 52, No. 4

To Monsieur Nicolas Rubinstein

Prelude and Fugue in A major

Op. 52, No. 5

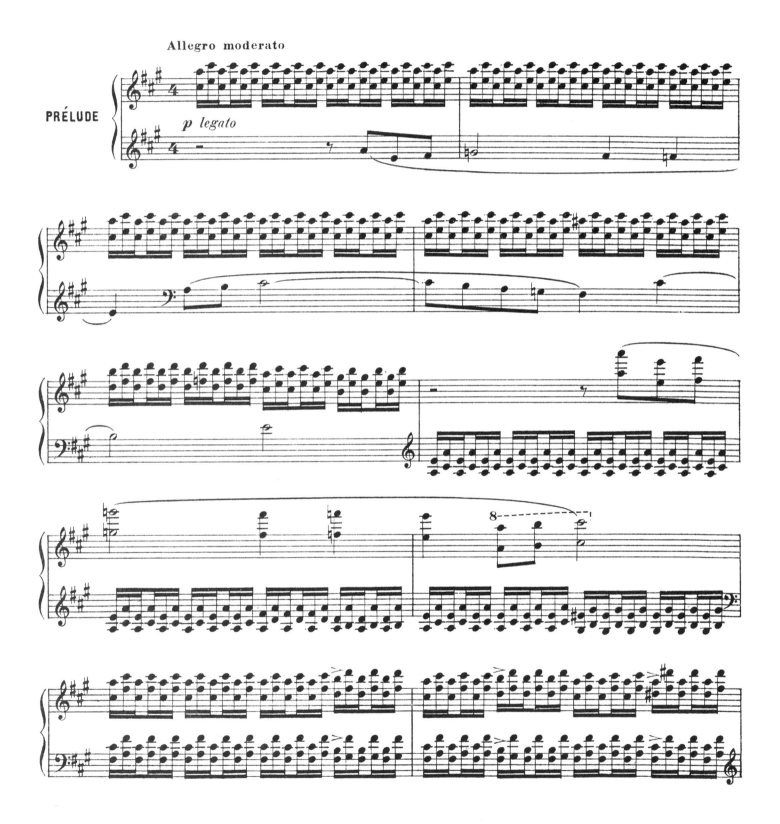

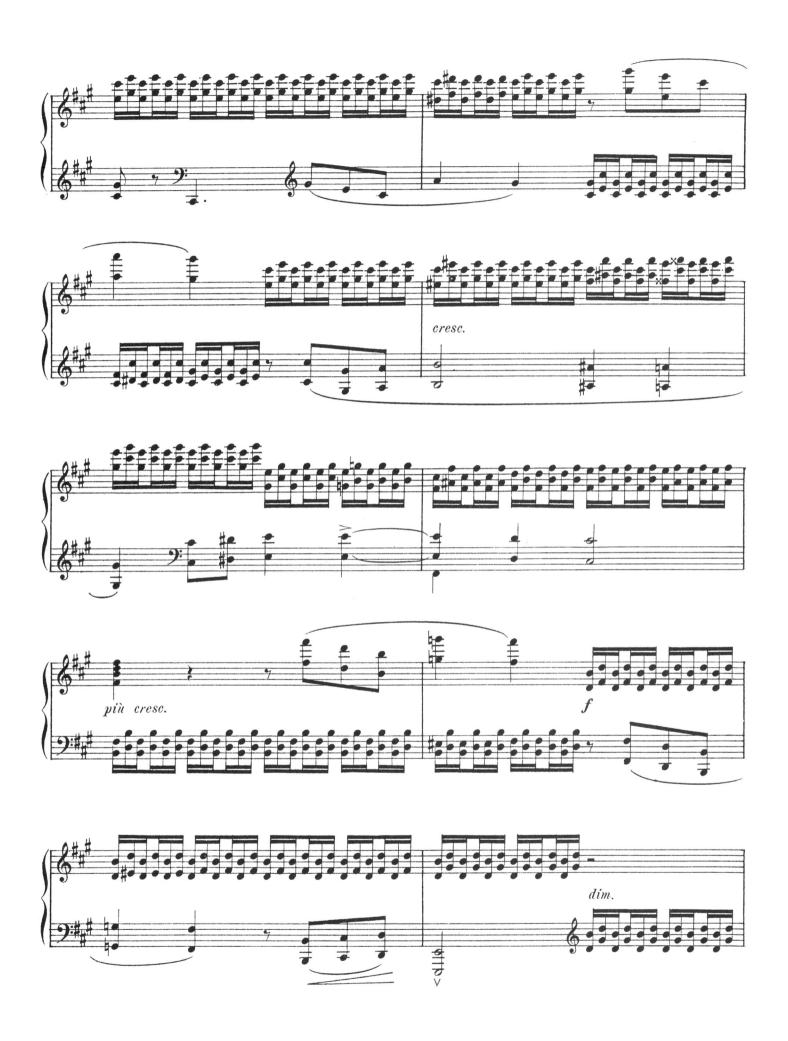

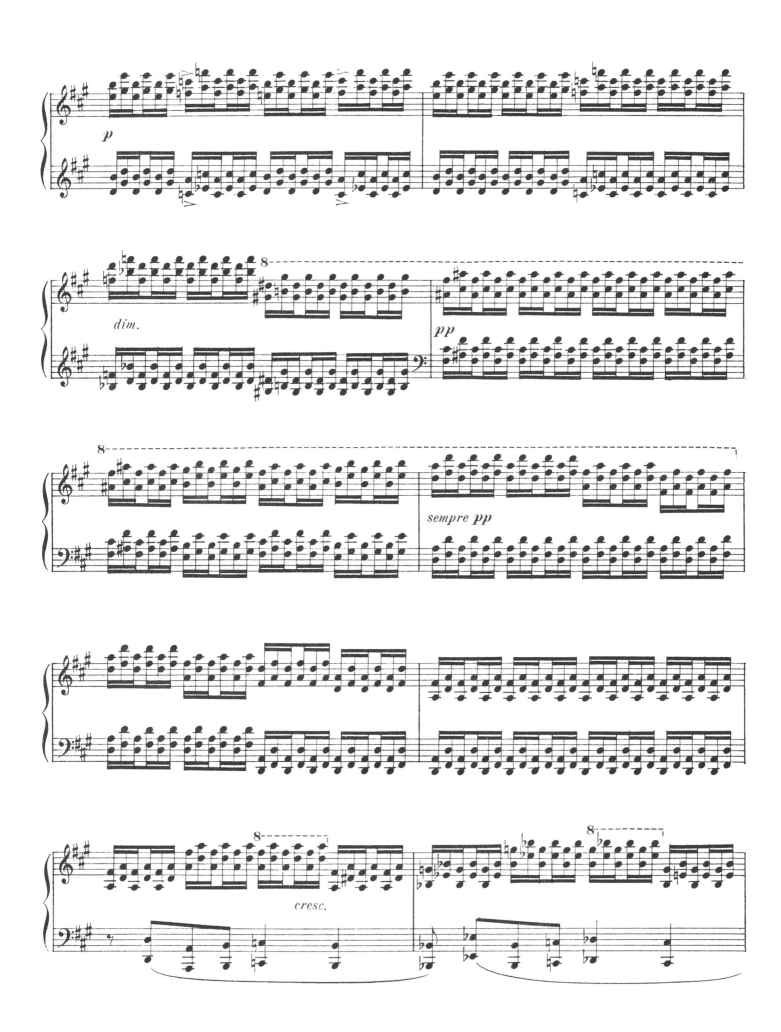

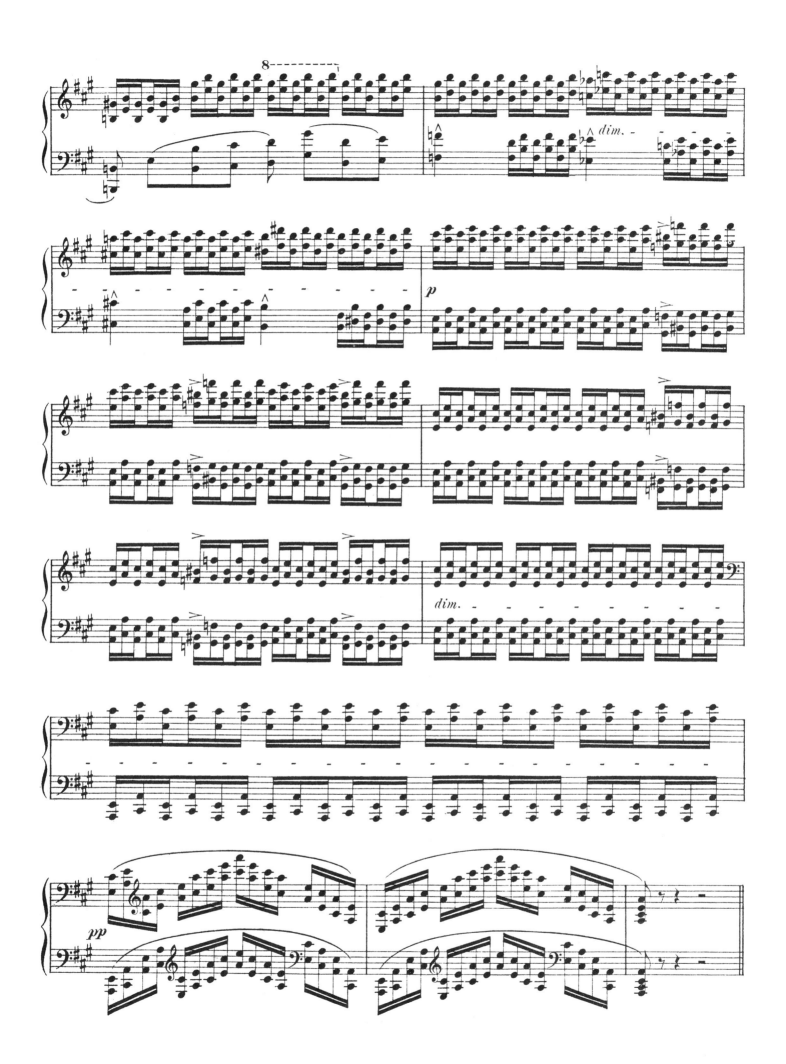

FUGUE

To Madame Marie Jaëll

En forme de valse

In waltz form • Op. 52, No. 6

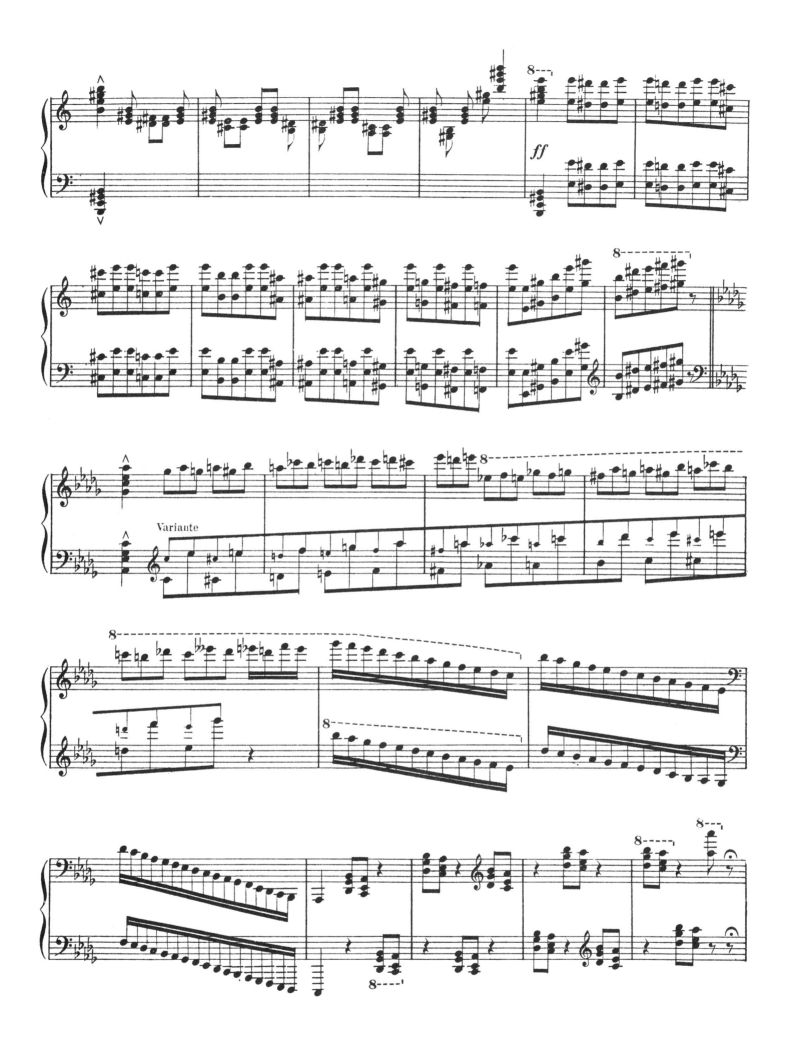

Allegro appassionato

Op. 70 (1884)

66   *Allegro appassionato*

Allegro appassionato

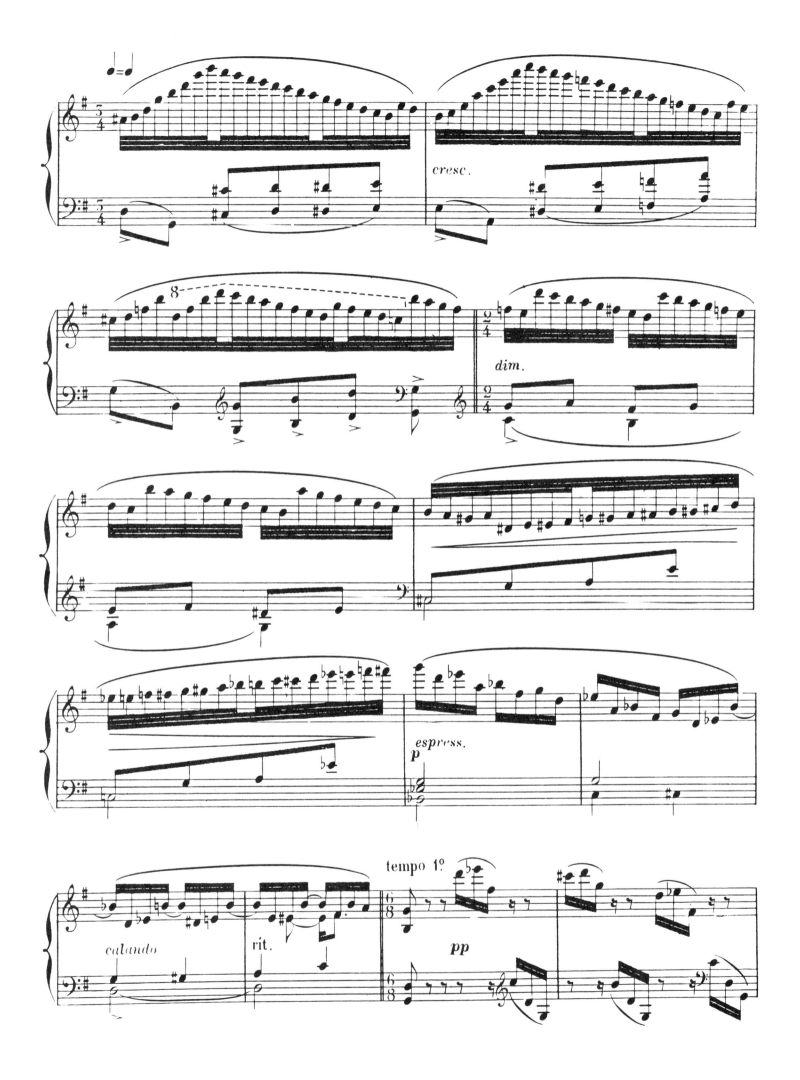

72   *Allegro appassionato*

ALBUM POUR PIANO

Piano album • Op. 72 (1884)

To Mademoiselle Anna Hoskier

Prélude

Op. 72, No. 1

Poco allegro, tempo rubato

Carillon

Op. 72, No. 2

Toccata

Op. 72, No. 3

Valse

Waltz • Op. 72, No. 4

Chanson napolitaine

Neapolitan song • Op. 72, No. 5

Finale

Op. 72, No. 6

Rhapsodie d'Auvergne

Auvergne rhapsody • Op. 73 (1884)

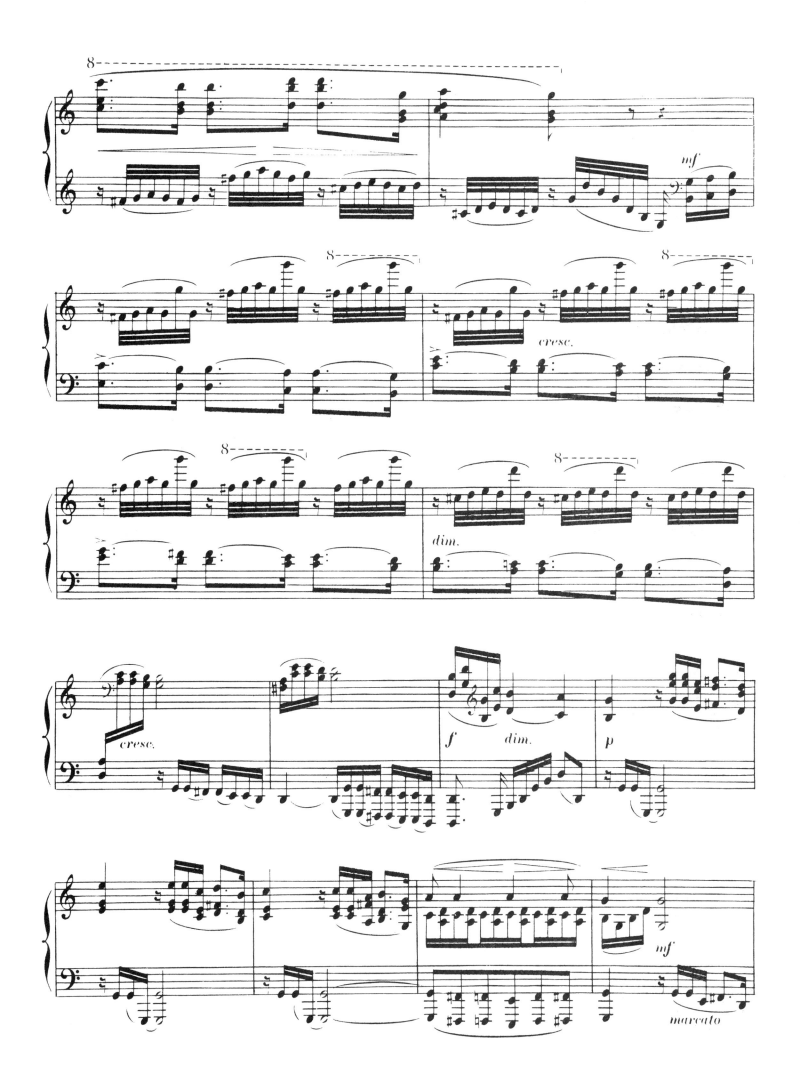

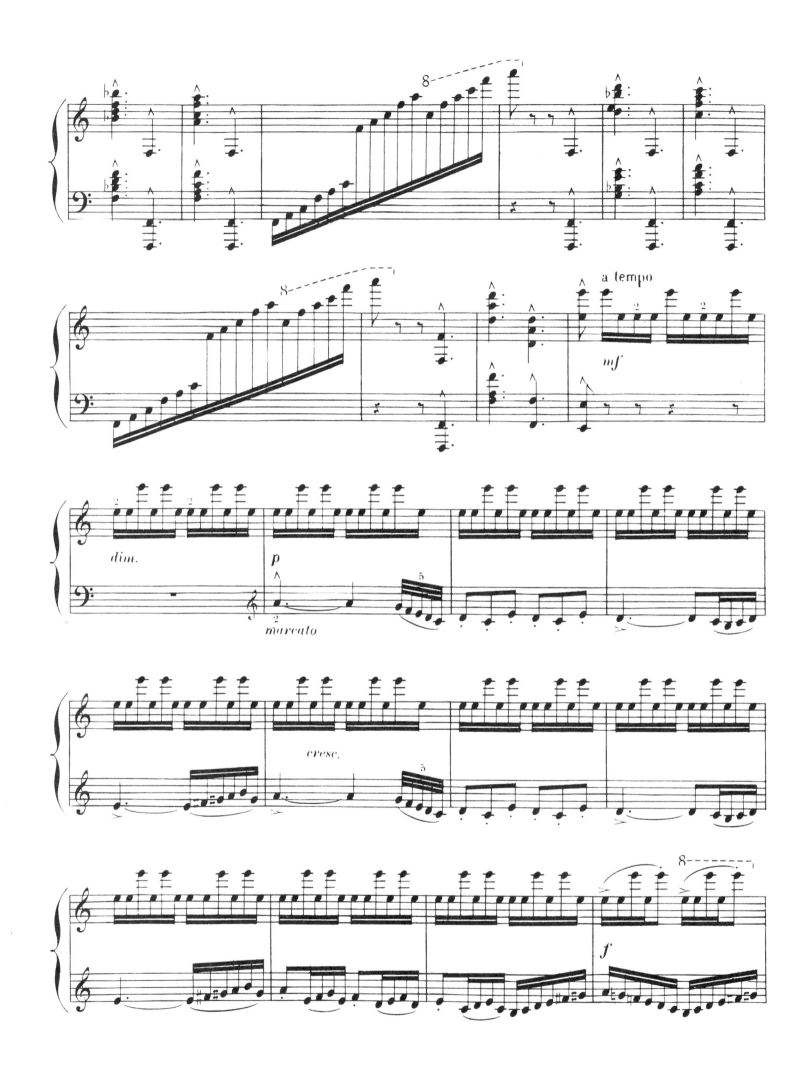

Wedding Cake
Caprice-Valse

Op. 76 (1885)

Originally for piano and orchestra / Transcribed for solo piano by A. Benfeld

marcato il canto

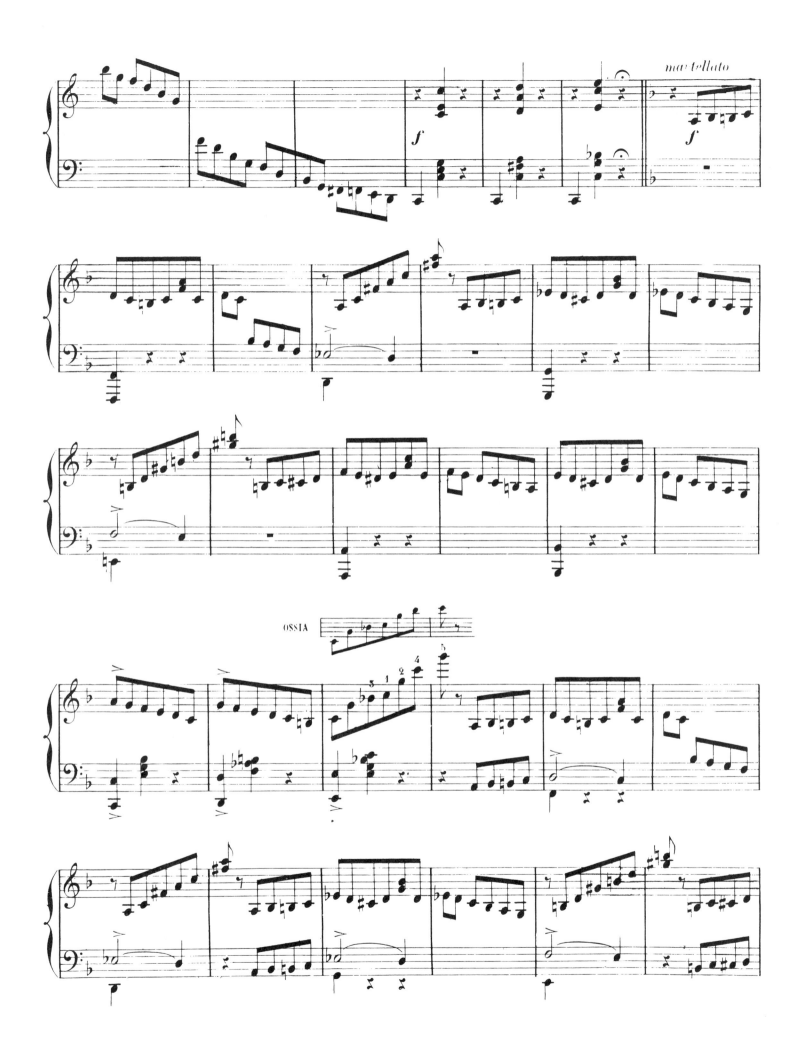

Thême varié

Varied theme • Op. 97 (1894)

Written for the Conservatory Competitions

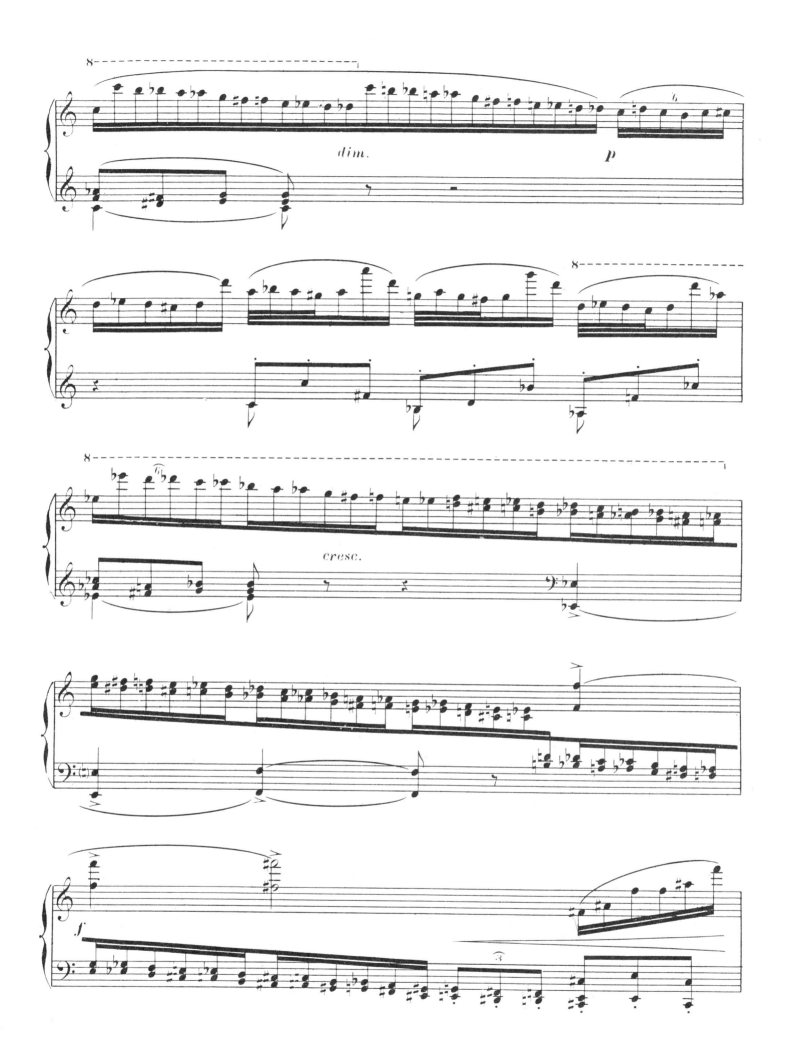

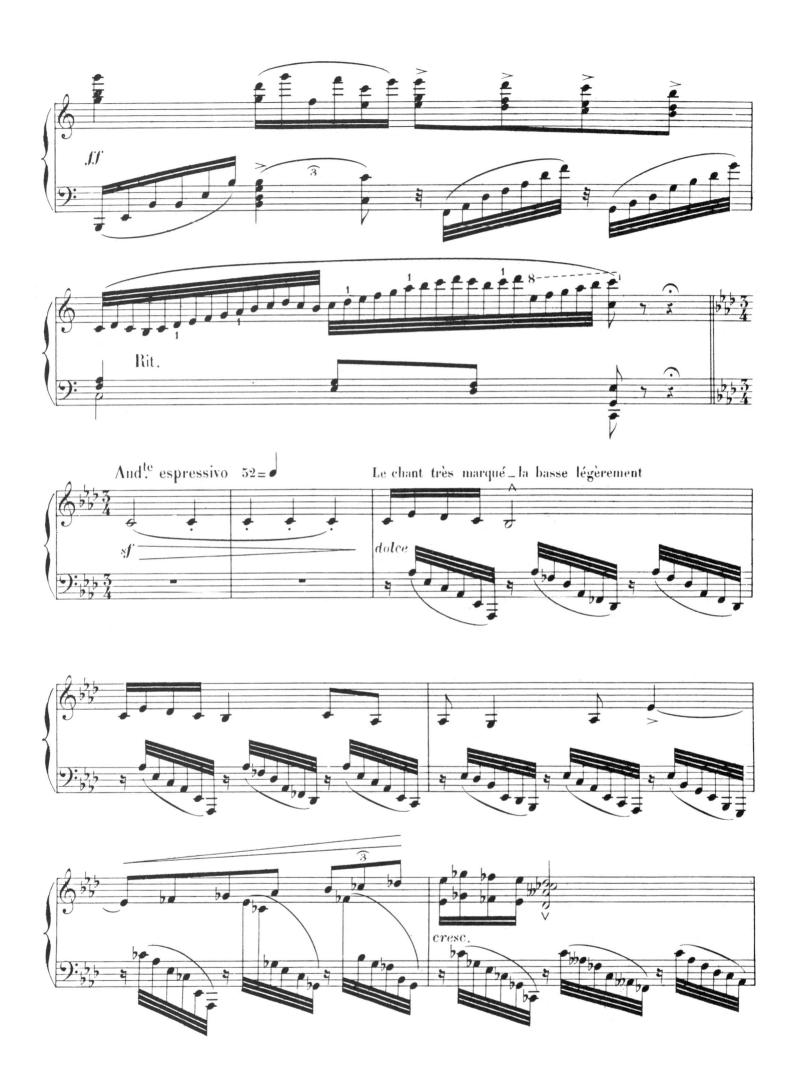

Thême varié

To Her Highness the Princess Bedia Osman

Valse mignonne

Delicate waltz • Op. 104 (1896)

172   *Valse mignonne*

Valse langoureuse

Languid waltz • Op. 120 (1903)

Allegretto vivace

Accelerando

Valse gaie

Gay waltz • Op. 139 (1913)

(sans Pédale)

dim.

pp

p

Ped.

8- -

cresc.

f

Three pieces from

SIX ÉTUDES POUR LE PIANO

Six piano studies • Op. 111 (1899)

To Monsieur Charles Malherbe

Prelude and Fugue in E-flat minor

Op. 111, No. 3

To Mademoiselle Clotilde Kleeberg

"Les cloches de Las Palmas"

"The bells of Las Palmas" • Op. 111, No. 4

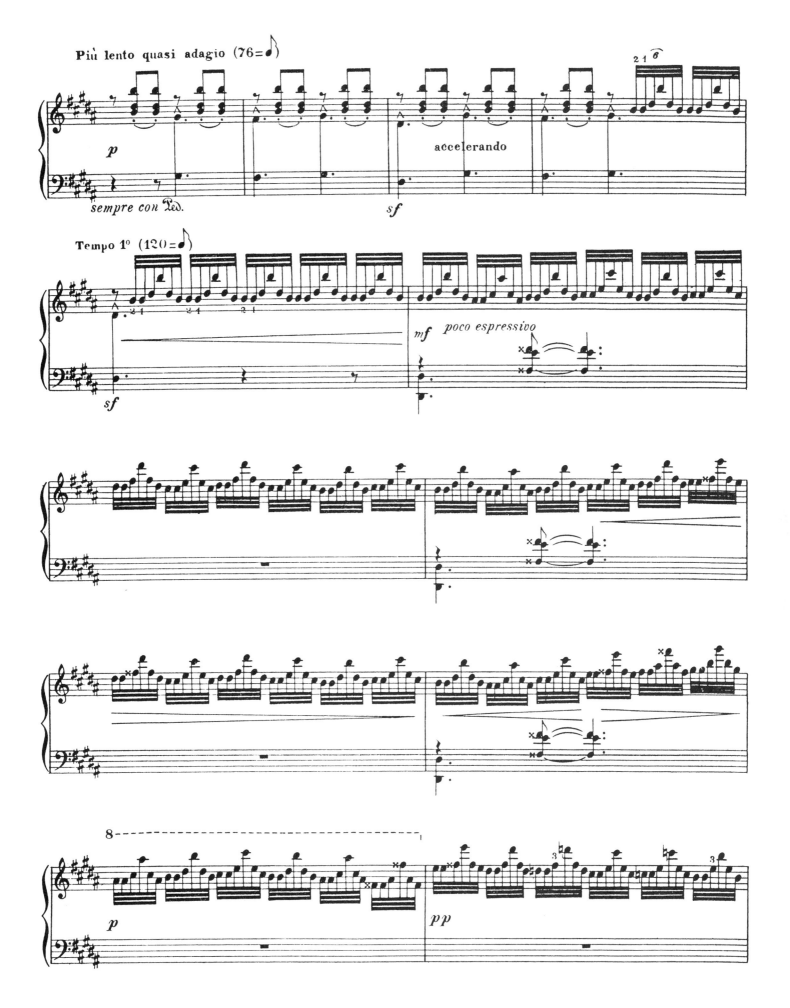

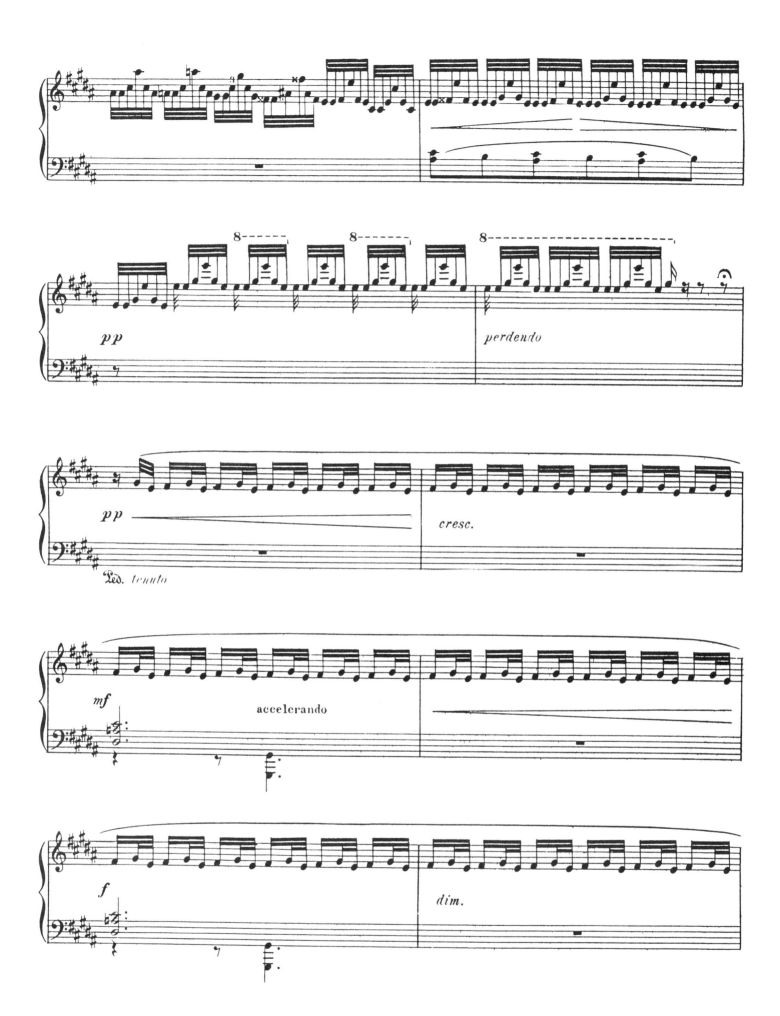

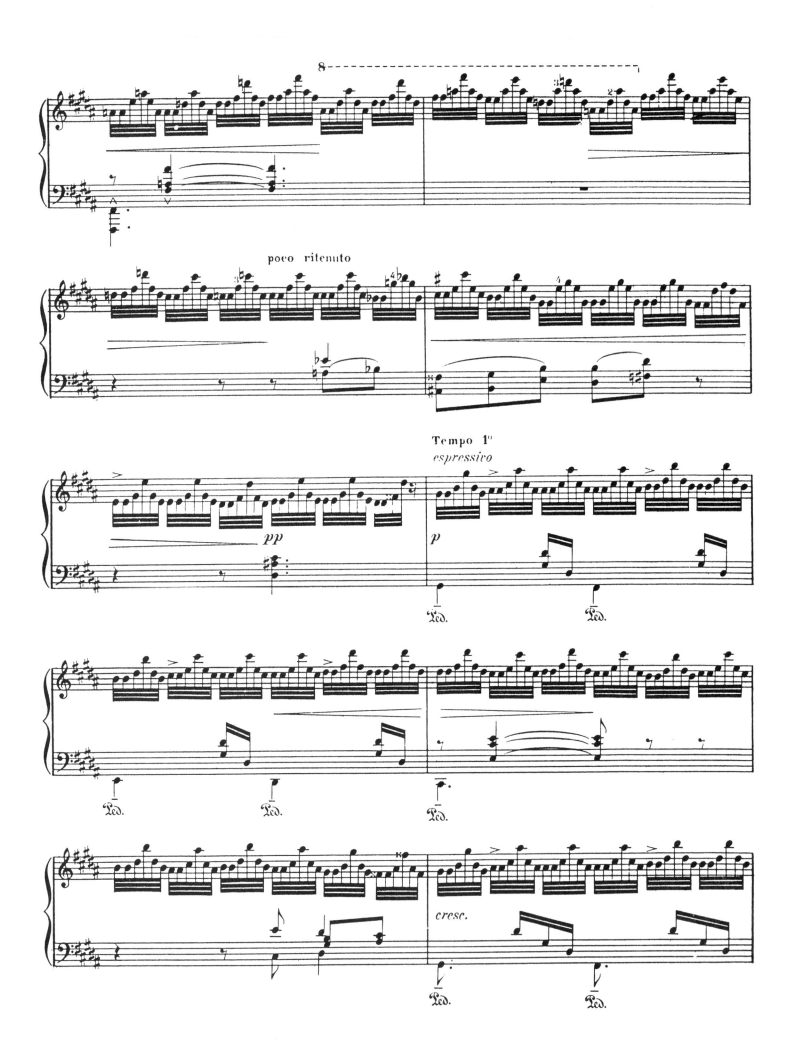

To Monsieur Raoul Pugno

Toccata

Op. 111, No. 6

After the Finale of the 5th Piano Concerto

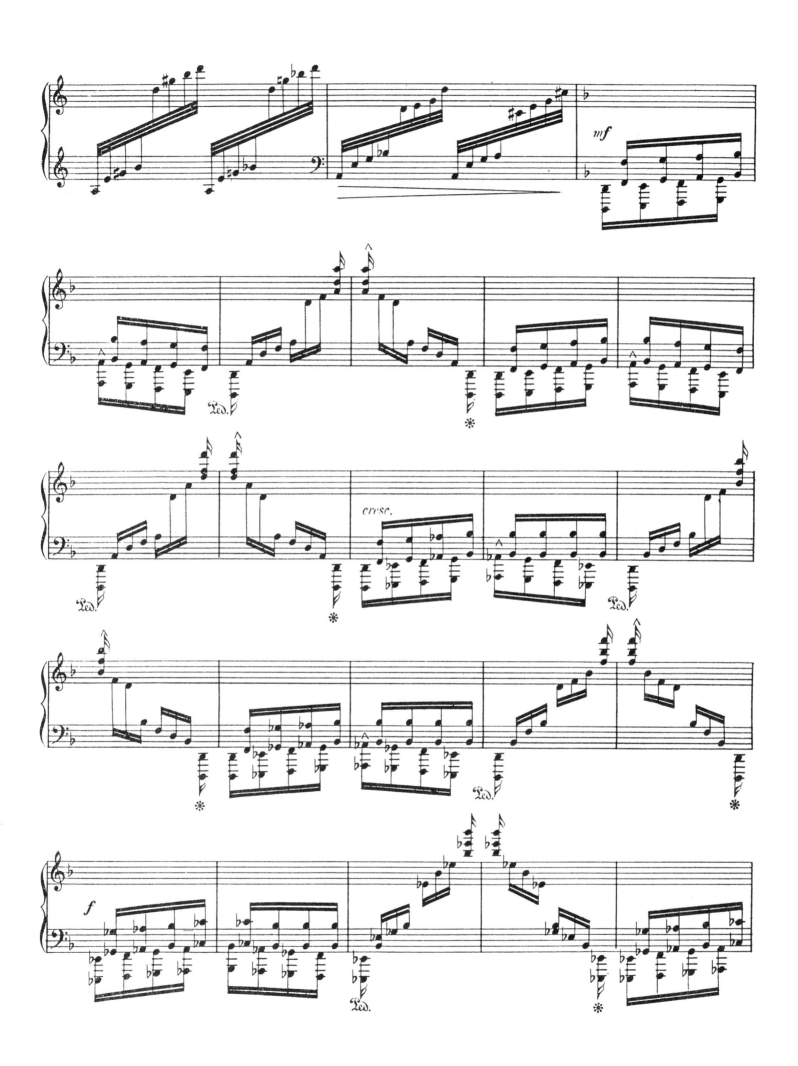

SIX ÉTUDES
POUR LA MAIN GAUCHE SEULE

Six studies for left hand alone • Op. 135 (1912)

To Madame Caroline de Serres (Montigny-Rémaury)

Prélude

Op. 135, No. 1

Six études pour la main gauche

Alla fuga

In fugal style • Op. 135, No. 2

Moto perpetuo

Perpetual motion • Op. 135, No. 3

Allegretto. Doux et tranquille. *sans vitesse et très également.*

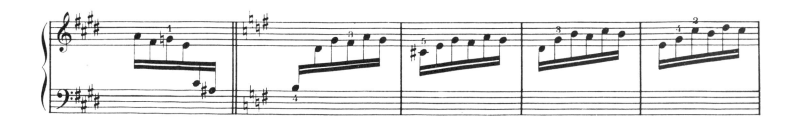

Six études pour la main gauche

Bourrée

Op. 135, No. 4

Six études pour la main gauche

non legato

cresc.

f

ff

Ped.   Ped.

Ped.   Ped.   Ped.   Ped.   Ped.

Élégie

Elegy • Op. 135, No. 5

(1) *Cet accord ne doit pas être frappé.*

[This chord must not be struck.]

Gigue

Op. 135, No. 6

Six études pour la main gauche

END OF EDITION